SKETCHBOOK

MUSEE D'ORSAY
PARIS

STORIES, JOURNAL/COLORING BOOK
(A book you can make your own)

DEAMER DUNN

Sometimes the manner and passion that people look at and enjoy art is as interesting as the art itself. Join this adventure by making this book your own...

Copyright © 2025 Deamer Dunn
All rights reserved. No part of this publication may be reproduced in any form or by any means without written permission from the publishers Deamer Dunn and Pajaro Street Publishing

Available to resellers through:

KDP PUBLISHING
ISBN-13: 9798386090500

INGRAM PUBLISHING
ISBN-13: 9798349257162

Editor: Dani Cyrer

All Art by Deamer

First Addition
Pajaro Street Inc

SKETCHBOOK – PARIS MUSEE D'ORSAY

Book Notes & Disclosures

Most of my sketch victims were unaware that my camera, eye and pencil clad fingers had focused upon them. For the most part, the tales I write for this series of sketchbooks are on individuals I know nothing of, beyond what I observed from drawing them. Consider these as bonus material for inspiring you to make this book your own.

I also published two additional Paris books. In my sketchbook series, 'SKETCHBOOK PARIS.' The drawings in this book are organized by their corresponding Paris arrondissement. Fourteen of these neighborhoods are represented.

For most of my sketchbook locations, I also create a novel for my recurring chef character. OMAR T IN PARIS: Chef Omar heads to the city of love to help with the food service for the film, 'Paris Fourteen.' This collection of short films is shot in each of the first 12 Paris arrondissements as well as the 14th & 18th. Romance blossoms on and off screen. ABOUT THE SERIES: Omar and his family travel to a different location for each of these culinary adventures. The travel fiction aspect is enhanced with descriptions of actual sites, restaurants, bookstores, galleries and shops—including sketches, favorite lists and recipes. Diversity in race, religion, culture, language and sexual orientation not only exists within Omar's family, it is celebrated in these tales. Each Omar T book is independent, you do not need to read them in the order of their publication, though, as the collection grows, there are more references between the novels.

ENJOY!

Artist/Author Deamer Dunn
Author Web Site: http://artbz.bz
Amazon Author Page: https://www.amazon.com/author/deamerdunn
(Please pass on your impressions; write a review on Amazon and/or other sites)
You can also support your local bookstore via: https://bookshop.org/shop/deamerdunn

YouTube Author/Artist Page (music videos of art & book sketches):
https://www.youtube.com/user/deamerdunn
https://www.instagram.com/deamerauthor/
Friend me on Facebook: Deamer Dunn Author
I would love to hear from you: deamer@artbz.bz

As a Journal/Coloring Book:
A BOOK YOU CAN MAKE YOUR OWN

DEAMER Sketchbooks hope to inspire the creative child in you. In case you haven't heard, coloring books for all ages are becoming quite a passion. Perhaps our ever-complicated world and its demands on our attention are fueling this trend. I think that we all wish that we had more time for reading. For many, perhaps a little coloring can still feed a passion for getting into a book and more easily allow the satisfaction of finishing something. Not only is this book designed to be fun as a coloring book, it is also laid out in a journal format. By leaving you a blank page with each drawing, the idea is you can add your own thoughts, ideas and images. Why settle for a blank book to keep track of life when you can associate your thoughts with an image—a sketch that you can also add your own color to? The idea is that this is a book that you can make your own. This series also hopes to be a supplement for travel. Whether you take it along or you allow it to take you.

Cheers! *Salud! A Votre Sante! Saluti!*

My hope is that this book will assist you in expanding the artistic experience of the Musée D'Orsay. Whether you take this book along as you explore the D'Orsay and its works of art, or if you let Sketchbook D'Orsay take you inside of the museum. Rather than overly organize these sketches, I decided to lay them out in the order I drew them. I assigned a few labels for context. But, consider these drawings as a device for a treasure hunt. Whether or not, you wish to see how many of these depicted works you can find and/or recognize from their historic exposure. I hope to inspire you to add color and/or add to the blank pages. Whether you are at home or sitting in the museum next to one of the depicted artworks. In other words, personalize your visit to the Museum D'Orsay and/or continue the experience over a café au lait or on your plane ride back home. While you take in a scene. Maybe you will be inspired to write a story of your own, or add some poetic words. Perhaps, you will come to the same realization as this artist, that observing those examining historic art is just as interesting as the artworks themselves…

SKETCHBOOK – PARIS MUSEE D'ORSAY

Index

IMAGES WITH STORIES:
6-7   Sharing my Love of Art
8-9   Selfie
10-11 First Date
12-13 Women in Art
14-15 Neighboring Cafés
IMAGES & BLANK PAGES FOR YOU
17-181

182   APPENDIX OF IMAGES
184   DEAMER BOOKS
189   ABOUT THE AUTHOR

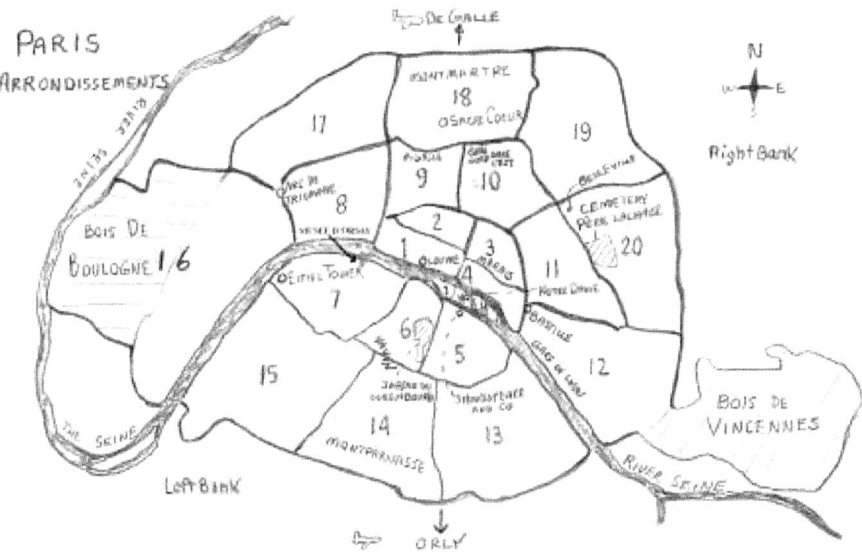

Sharing my Love of Art

Despite the impatient drive of his youth, my son relented to the idea of spending an afternoon in a museum with me. To my delight, once we were inside the Musée D'Orsay, he rallied around my passion toward the art. His attitude changed quickly once we made it inside and walked into its center. The spectacular high arching glass ceiling of the former rail station is a real attention grabber. The D'Orsay's collection of 19th and 20th century art is particularly interesting to me, so I hoped to spend as long as possible to share my love with my son. I took advantage of their audio program so I could pass along accurate information to my boy. This turned out to be a great idea, as he accepted the information, instead of doubting everything that his ma had to say. The museum's mix of paintings and sculpture stroked his attention. Also, the sense of discovery from room to room seemed to help keep his interest. My boy's reaction to the paintings of Vincent Van Gogh was really pleasing. Something about Van Gogh's style really appealed to his blossoming brain. He commanded that I take a picture of him next to 'La Nuit étoilée sur le Rhône. I felt some extra emotion when he wasn't satisfied with my first image. My heart jumped as he commanded, "Take another one mom." As he stood so perfectly still, something I rarely see, I was really touched. His expression and connection to a piece of art of a previous century, was priceless to me. As we were leaving this great Paris sanctuary, my eyes got a little glossy. I had this vision of him returning with his child, seeking our Van Gogh together, and my grandchild standing still so his Dad could capture the moment in a photograph of his own.

First Date

I had my eye on Marie for quite some time. We have a couple of classes together at the Sorbonne. It took me a while to discern whether she was aloof or just shy. I got the feeling she was new to Paris, from somewhere in the provinces. The big breakthrough came when I encountered her in the study hall with a book on 20th century art. This set me up perfectly to ask her if she had yet been to the Musée D'Orsay. She just shook her head back and forth in the negative. "*Incroyable*," I exclaimed. "You must let me take you, it is one of my favorite places in the world!" Her blossoming red face let me know the degree of her shyness. I sat down and started to flip through the pages pointing out this and that painting that I knew were in the sacred walls of the D'Orsay. Her passion toward the art of this time pushed away her timidness and brought confidence to her eyes as she started to add knowledge to our discussion.

It still took several weeks before she finally agreed to let me lead her into the hallow ground of this spectacular museum. She remained very timid and not very talkative on our walk along the river Seine until we were inside. Her cheeks turned red again when we were in front of a Renoir nude, which I found wonderfully adorable. Funny how a display of nudity can add something awkward to a first date…

It was equally thrilling as she became more comfortable, as her love of art history pushed her shyness to the back of her brain. She even agreed to having lunch with me in the restaurant, 'but only if we go Dutch, I insist on paying for my own." Over some paté, salad and a glass of Sancerre, we shared our upbringing stories. The second best moment of our day was when little miss shy girl suddenly couldn't stop talking. The best was when we were walking back to school and she slipped her hand into mine.

SKETCHBOOK – PARIS MUSEE D'ORSAY

Women in Art

As a woman, I always felt a special connection to the impressionist painters Mary Cassett and Berthe Morisot. Like so many, the iconic paintings of this era spoke to my emotions. The work of these two ladies particularly caught my attention. They were the first women I ever noticed being mentioned in the elemental history classes of my youth that were actually a part of a movement, a moment in time. Once I made it to college and studied women's literature, I particularly connected to the writings of Parisian Simone de Beauvoir. Her efforts to breakdown and intellectually discuss the woman condition made me see the world in a whole different light. I was also touched by her relationship with Jean-Paul Satre. Especially how they collaborated, loved and lived in each other's light but never married or had kids, while staying friends their whole lives—perhaps the greatest literary couple in history, now laying in rest next to each other in Cimetière du Montparnasse—very romantic. In fact, as my husband and I trooped though the D'Orsay sharing the experience, I thought if not for these three women, two with passionate paint and one of passionate pen, I might never had held out for the right man, a good man. A man who became my husband. A male who respects me for who I am and considers my gender his equal.

SKETCHBOOK – PARIS MUSEE D'ORSAY

Selfie

Following a visit to Musée D'Orsay, I had a most vivid dream. I dreamed that I was so inspired by the artwork of Vincent Van Gogh that I took up painting. In the dream I was a natural, colors instantly blended together to express flowers, cozy homes, fields and buildings in a manner perfected by the obsessed Dutchman adopted by the country of France. Unlike the troubled painter, my dream self was selling my paintings left and right. I was an overnight, pun intended, great success. But things changed in a dreamy scene of me a mirror and a canvas. The colors still flowed brilliantly as I worked on a self-portrait, but the omnipresent cocky emotions of my early dream success began to bend into disturbing emotions. What started as a stern confident pictorial face, started to misbehave. The eyes I had painted started to enlarge and take on an expression of fear or rage, maybe both. Then the sides of my head started to melt, as did my dream self. It all stayed colorful but all the shapes of my dream, turning into a nightmare, were blending together. The final visual I remember before the horror woke me was being inside my melting self, looking up from the puddle of color that was my former body. My eyes locked onto the canvas that I had been painting my Selfie, only to see three words emerging in blood red, 'My Ear Next.'

Neighboring Cafés

I'm aware that there are many who think of the French as being stuck-up, jaded. But I don't see it. Maybe because I was born and raised in Paris. This is our city, but we have always shared it with the world. This I find attractive, not bothersome. Okay, there are summer days when the number of tourists can be a bit overwhelming, but most of the time, I really appreciate our status with travelers. In fact, I take advantage of the stream of visitors to Paris. I live in the 7th arrondissement, not far from the Musée D'Orsay. One day I was loitering with a cup of café cream on the patio of Café D'Orsay, having fun trying to guess each new patron's country of origin. As someone who spends most the week inside a windowless cubical, enjoying our outdoor seating of our Parisian cafés is extra special. Though, this statement makes me laugh, since we Parisians think of our café experiences as essential as eating and sleeping…

Now, at least once a week, I take up residence at either Café D'Orsay or Café Deux Musée, with my coffee and my journal. I pick an individual, a couple or a group, guess their origin and make-up a story about them. The D'Orsay is such an inspiring museum that it brings the curious from every part of the globe. From the comfort of my seat, I'm entertained with a parade of the people of the world. I find it more entertaining than the museum itself. Anyway, time to head back to my cubical, though, with one more page of my journal filled…

SKETCHBOOK – PARIS MUSEE D'ORSAY

SKETCHBOOK – PARIS MUSEE D'ORSAY

SKETCHBOOK – PARIS MUSEE D'ORSAY

SKETCHBOOK – PARIS MUSEE D'ORSAY

SKETCHBOOK – PARIS MUSEE D'ORSAY

SKETCHBOOK – PARIS MUSEE D'ORSAY

SKETCHBOOK – PARIS MUSEE D'ORSAY

SKETCHBOOK – PARIS MUSEE D'ORSAY

SKETCHBOOK – PARIS MUSEE D'ORSAY

SKETCHBOOK – PARIS MUSEE D'ORSAY

SKETCHBOOK – PARIS MUSEE D'ORSAY

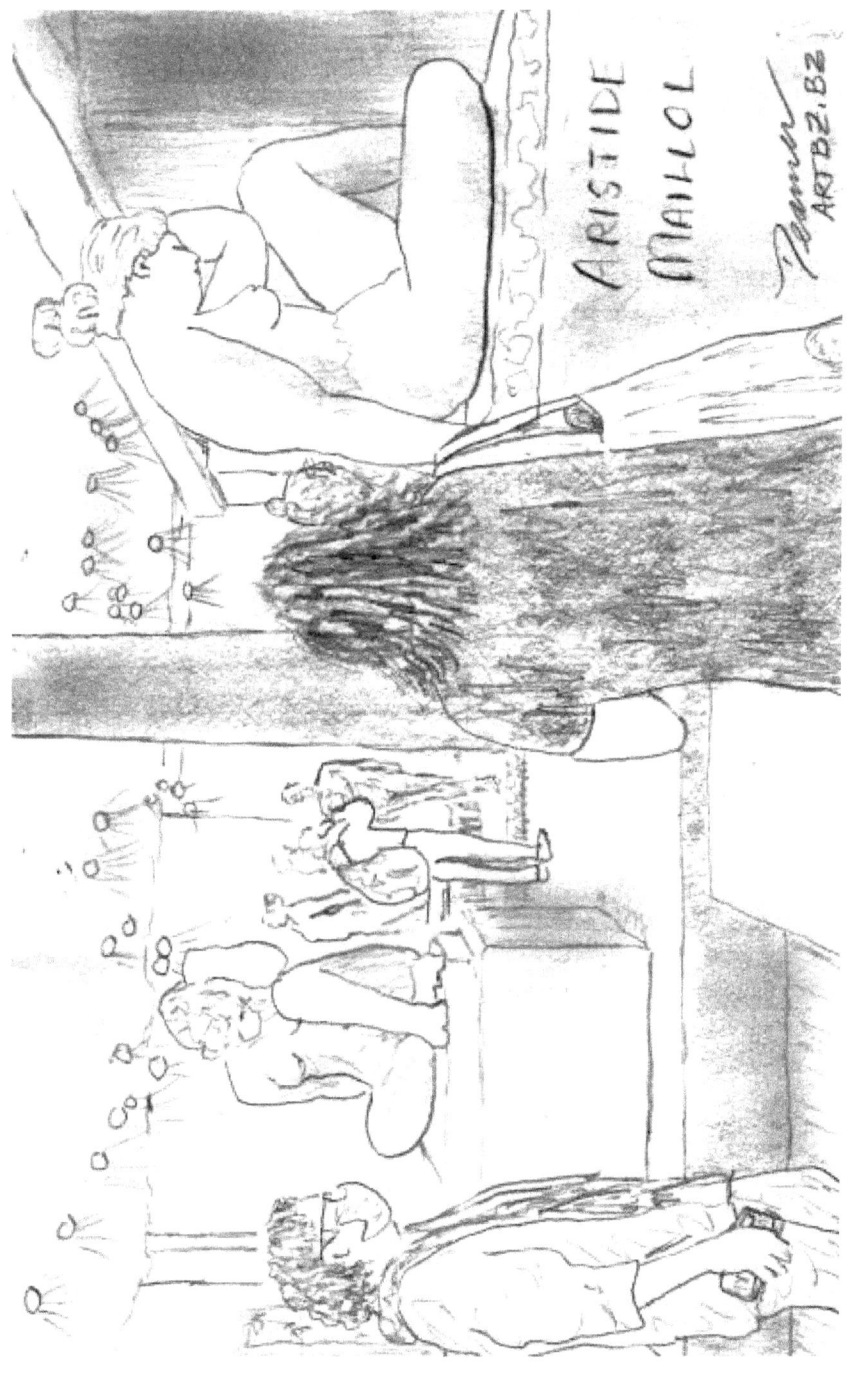

SKETCHBOOK – PARIS MUSEE D'ORSAY

SKETCHBOOK – PARIS MUSEE D'ORSAY

SKETCHBOOK – PARIS MUSEE D'ORSAY

SKETCHBOOK – PARIS MUSEE D'ORSAY

SKETCHBOOK – PARIS MUSEE D'ORSAY

SKETCHBOOK – PARIS MUSEE D'ORSAY

SKETCHBOOK – PARIS MUSEE D'ORSAY

SKETCHBOOK – PARIS MUSEE D'ORSAY

SKETCHBOOK – PARIS MUSEE D'ORSAY

SKETCHBOOK – PARIS MUSEE D'ORSAY

SKETCHBOOK – PARIS MUSEE D'ORSAY

SKETCHBOOK – PARIS MUSEE D'ORSAY

SKETCHBOOK – PARIS MUSEE D'ORSAY

SKETCHBOOK – PARIS MUSEE D'ORSAY

SKETCHBOOK – PARIS MUSEE D'ORSAY

SKETCHBOOK – PARIS MUSEE D'ORSAY

SKETCHBOOK – PARIS MUSEE D'ORSAY

SKETCHBOOK – PARIS MUSEE D'ORSAY

SKETCHBOOK – PARIS MUSEE D'ORSAY

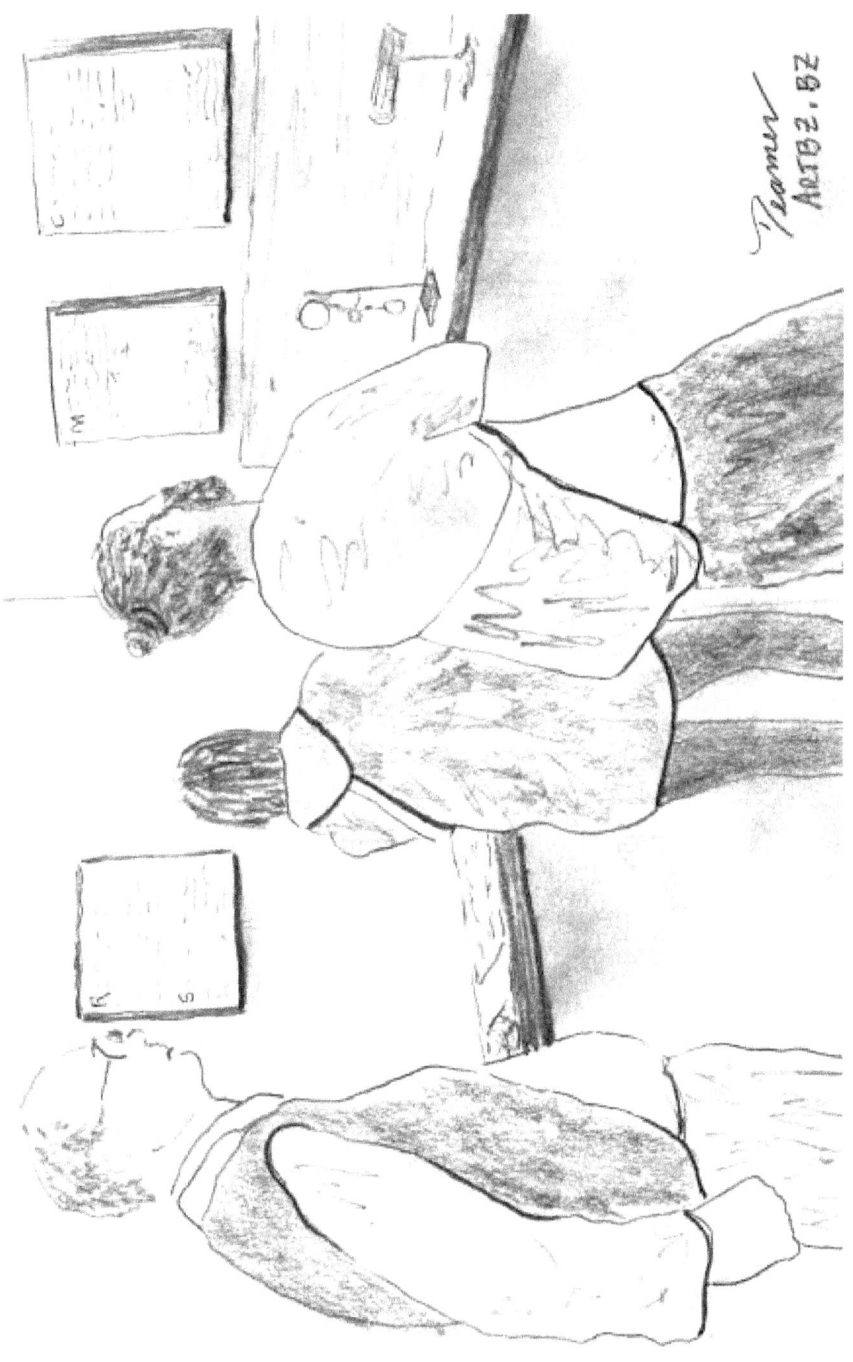

83

SKETCHBOOK – PARIS MUSEE D'ORSAY

SKETCHBOOK – PARIS MUSEE D'ORSAY

SKETCHBOOK – PARIS MUSEE D'ORSAY

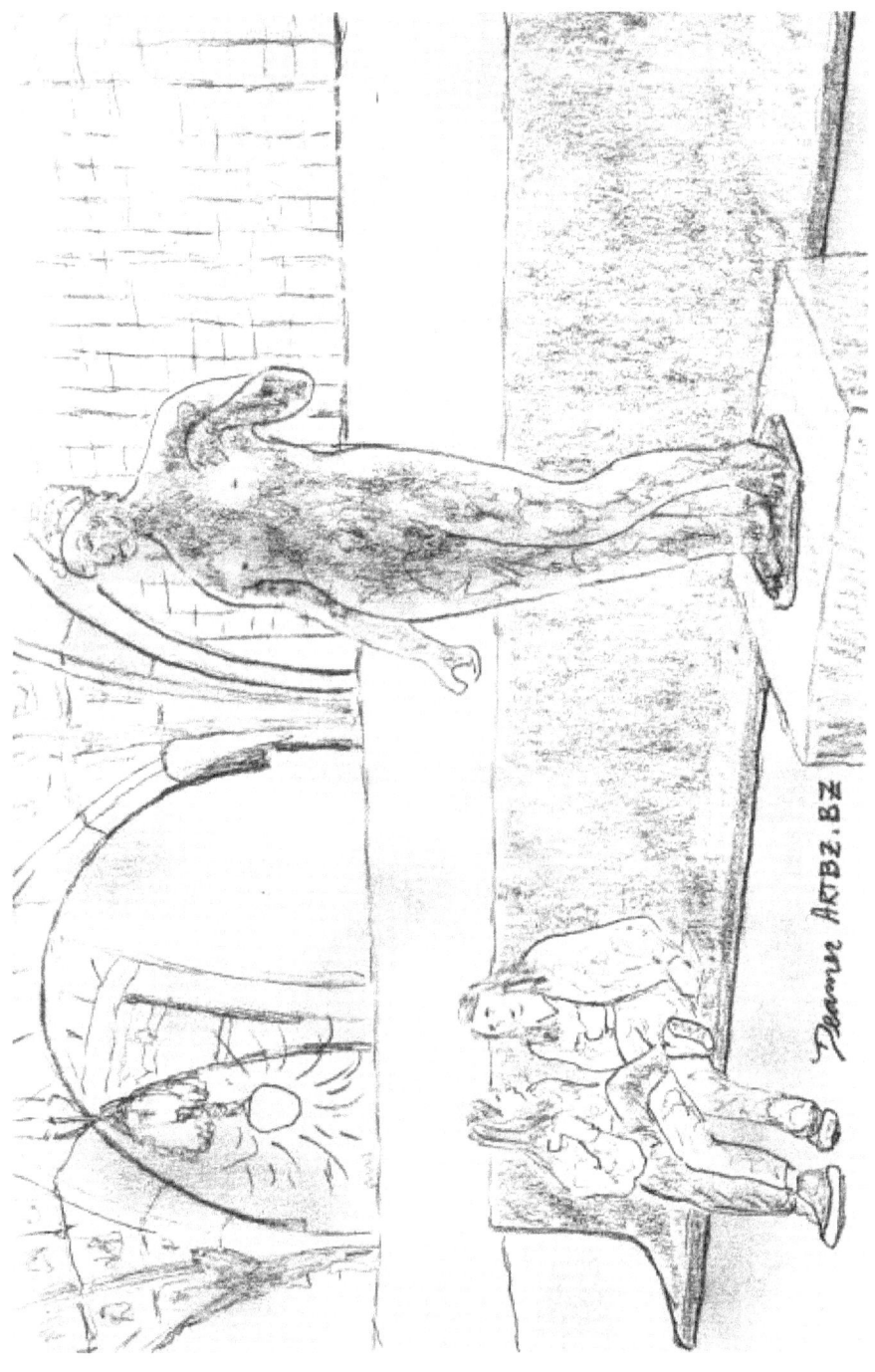

SKETCHBOOK – PARIS MUSEE D'ORSAY

SKETCHBOOK – PARIS MUSEE D'ORSAY

SKETCHBOOK – PARIS MUSEE D'ORSAY

SKETCHBOOK – PARIS MUSEE D'ORSAY

SKETCHBOOK – PARIS MUSEE D'ORSAY

SKETCHBOOK – PARIS MUSEE D'ORSAY

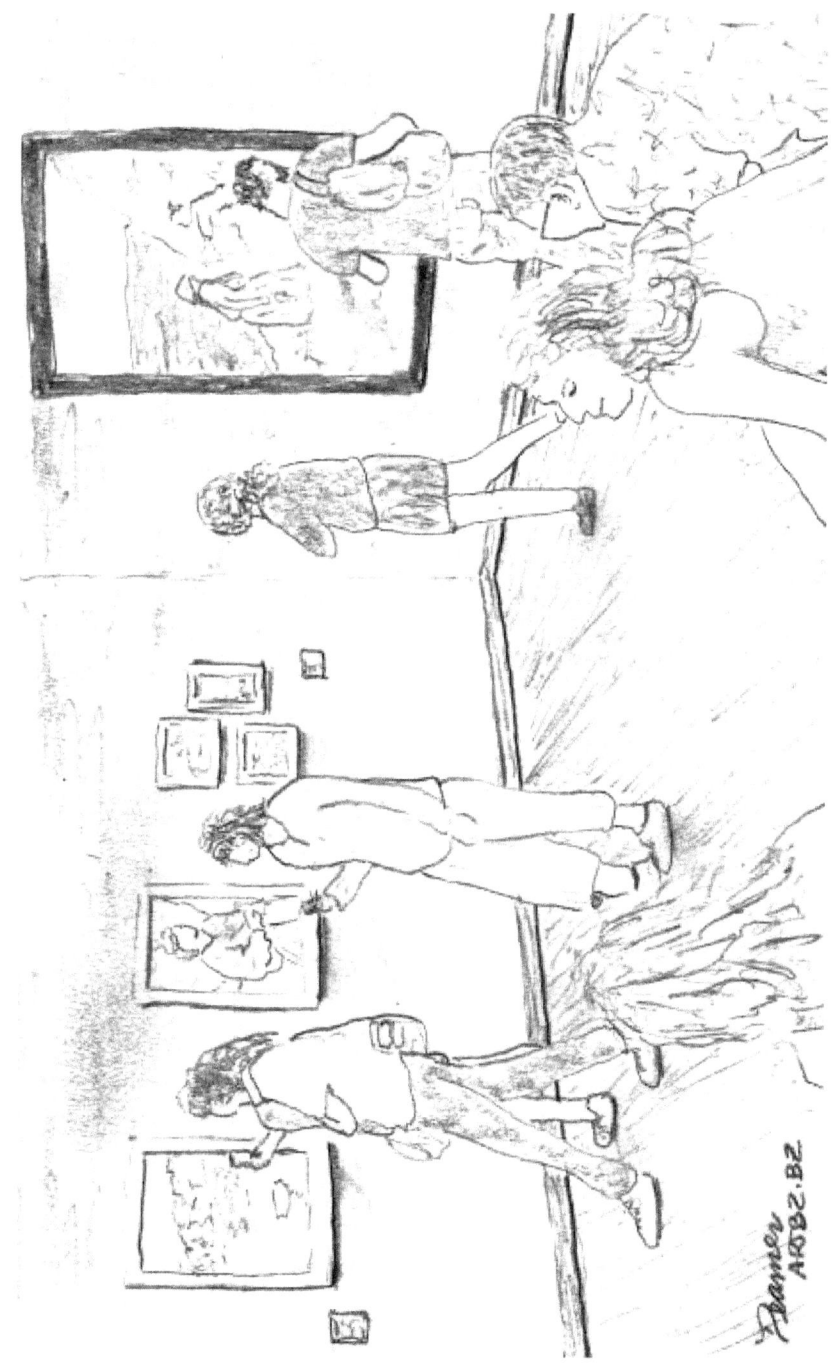

SKETCHBOOK – PARIS MUSEE D'ORSAY

SKETCHBOOK – PARIS MUSEE D'ORSAY

SKETCHBOOK – PARIS MUSEE D'ORSAY

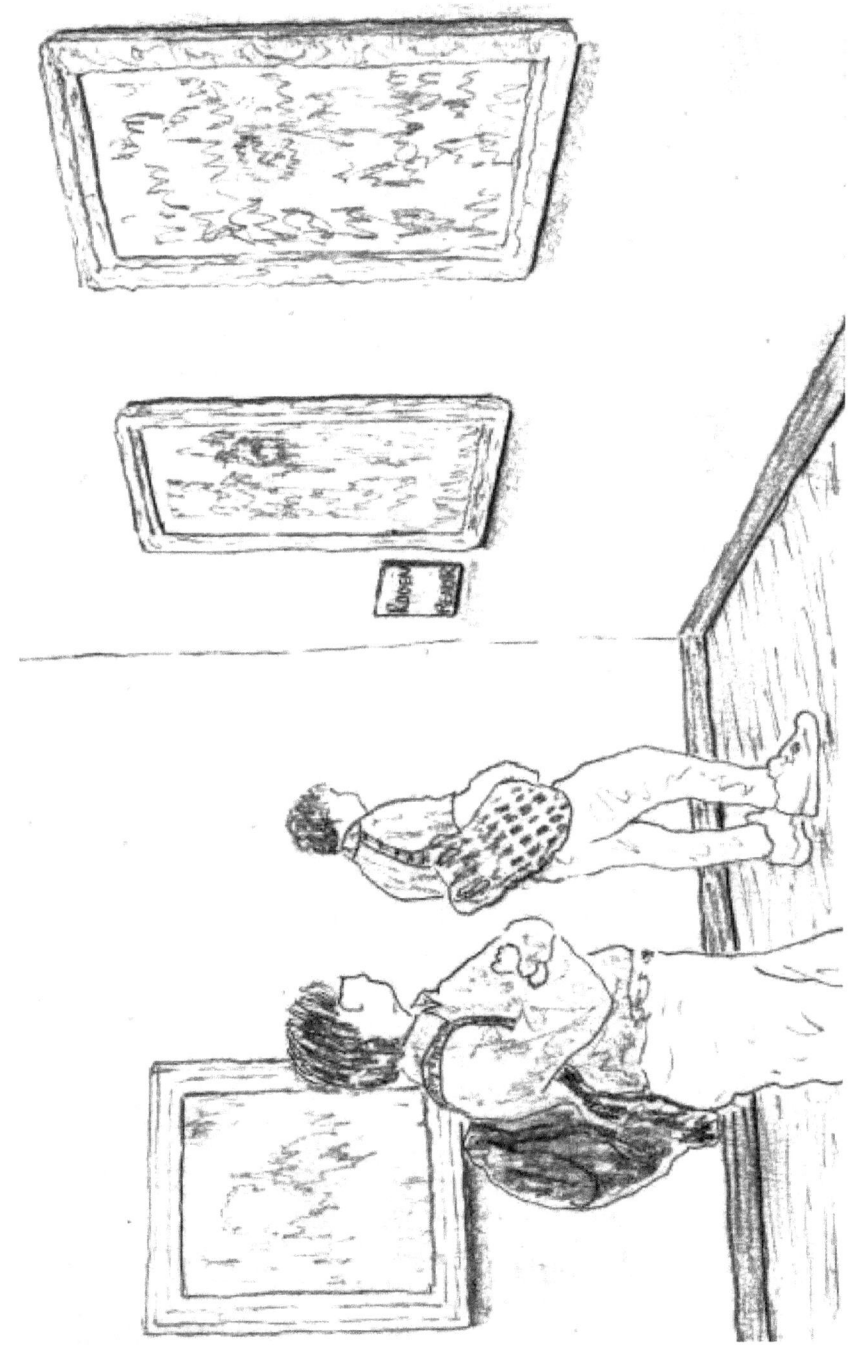

SKETCHBOOK – PARIS MUSEE D'ORSAY

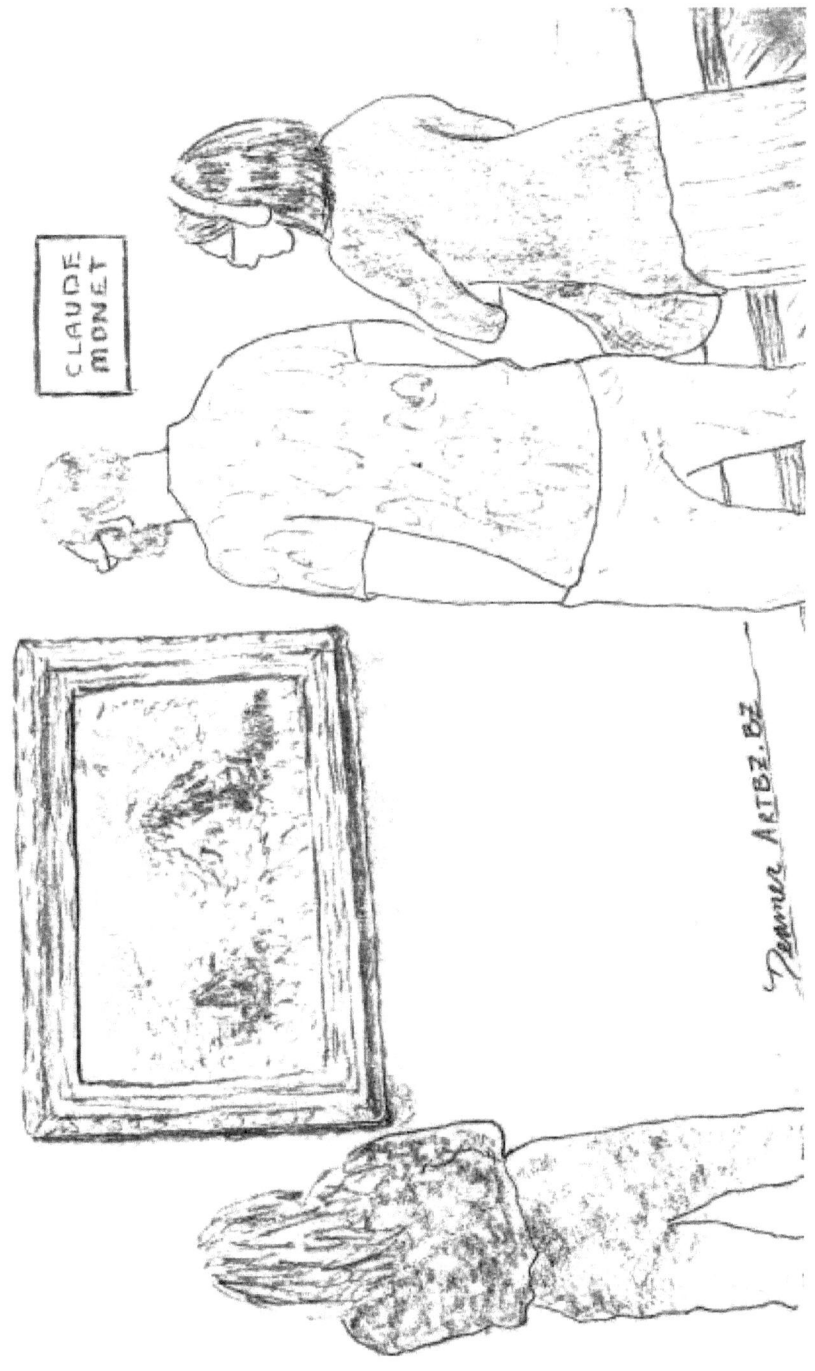

SKETCHBOOK – PARIS MUSEE D'ORSAY

SKETCHBOOK – PARIS MUSEE D'ORSAY

SKETCHBOOK – PARIS MUSEE D'ORSAY

SKETCHBOOK – PARIS MUSEE D'ORSAY

SKETCHBOOK – PARIS MUSEE D'ORSAY

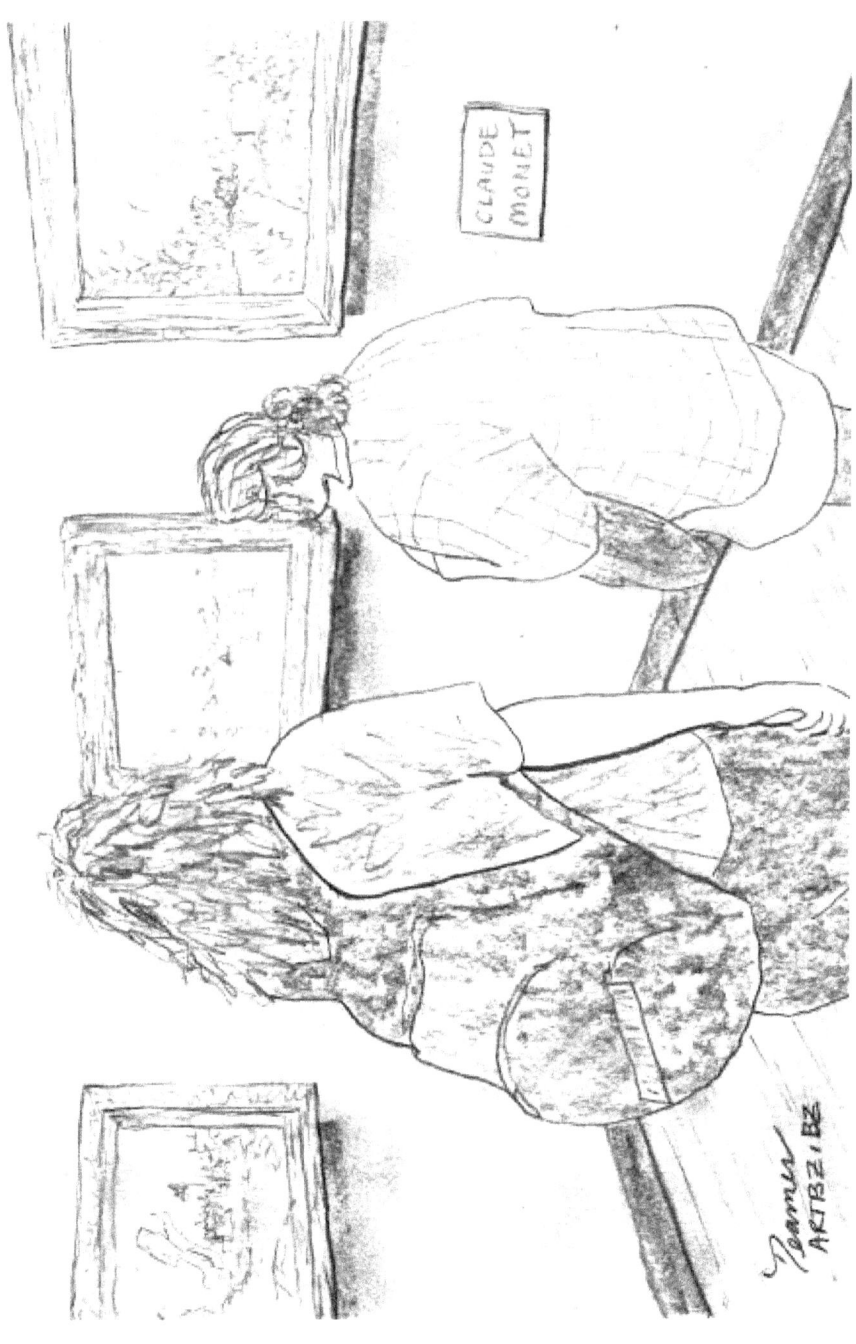

SKETCHBOOK – PARIS MUSEE D'ORSAY

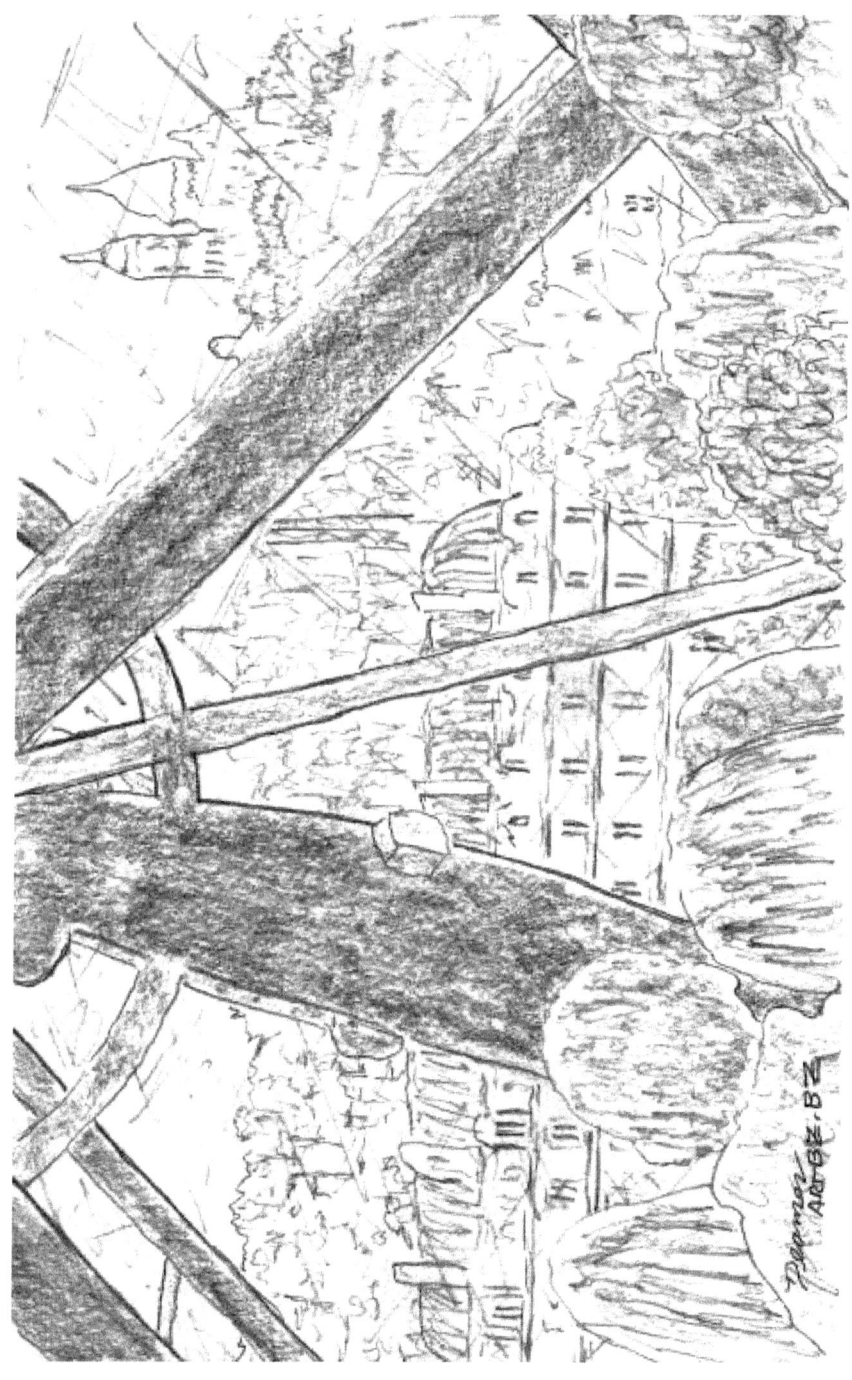

SKETCHBOOK – PARIS MUSEE D'ORSAY

SKETCHBOOK – PARIS MUSEE D'ORSAY

SKETCHBOOK – PARIS MUSEE D'ORSAY

SKETCHBOOK – PARIS MUSEE D'ORSAY

SKETCHBOOK – PARIS MUSEE D'ORSAY

SKETCHBOOK – PARIS MUSEE D'ORSAY

SKETCHBOOK – PARIS MUSEE D'ORSAY

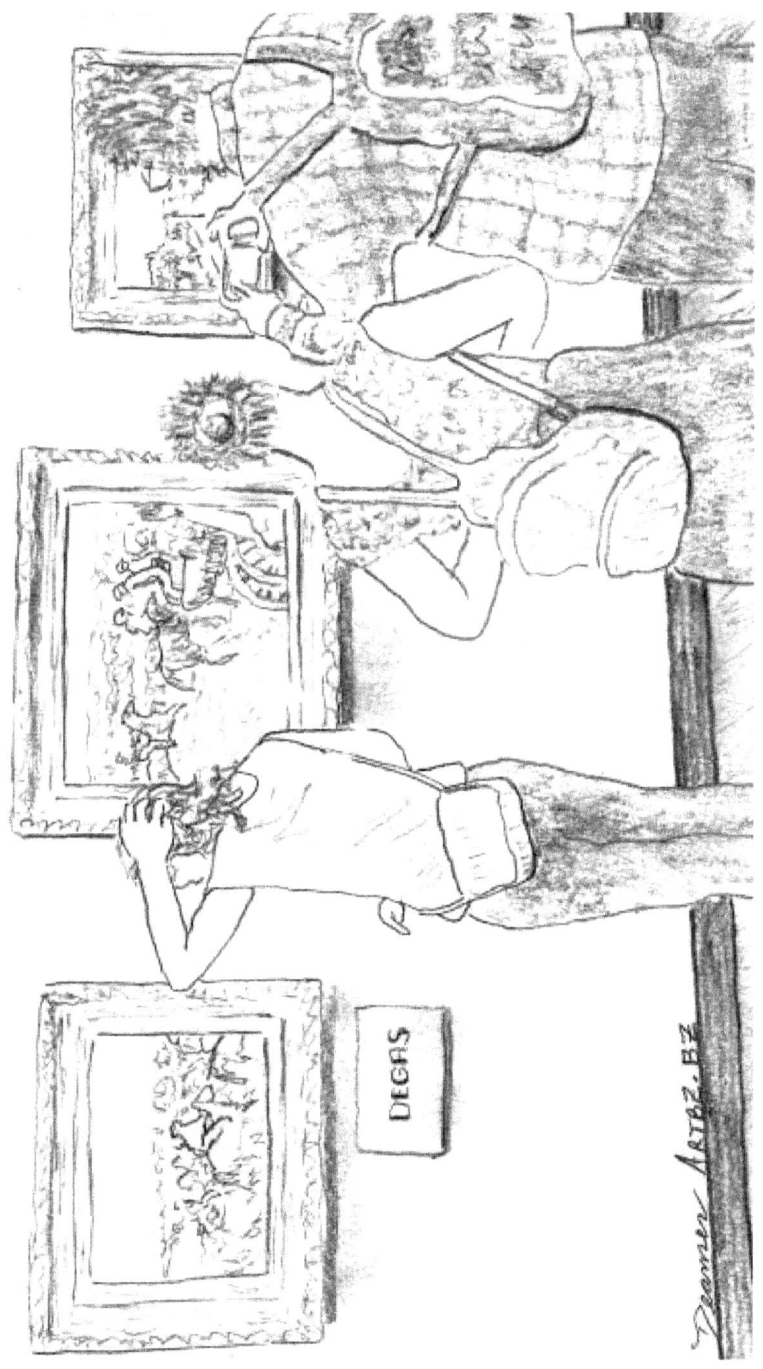

SKETCHBOOK – PARIS MUSEE D'ORSAY

SKETCHBOOK – PARIS MUSEE D'ORSAY

SKETCHBOOK – PARIS MUSEE D'ORSAY

SKETCHBOOK – PARIS MUSEE D'ORSAY

SKETCHBOOK – PARIS MUSEE D'ORSAY

155

SKETCHBOOK – PARIS MUSEE D'ORSAY

SKETCHBOOK – PARIS MUSEE D'ORSAY

SKETCHBOOK – PARIS MUSEE D'ORSAY

SKETCHBOOK – PARIS MUSEE D'ORSAY

165

SKETCHBOOK – PARIS MUSEE D'ORSAY

SKETCHBOOK – PARIS MUSEE D'ORSAY

SKETCHBOOK – PARIS MUSEE D'ORSAY

SKETCHBOOK – PARIS MUSEE D'ORSAY

SKETCHBOOK – PARIS MUSEE D'ORSAY

SKETCHBOOK – PARIS MUSEE D'ORSAY

SKETCHBOOK – PARIS MUSEE D'ORSAY

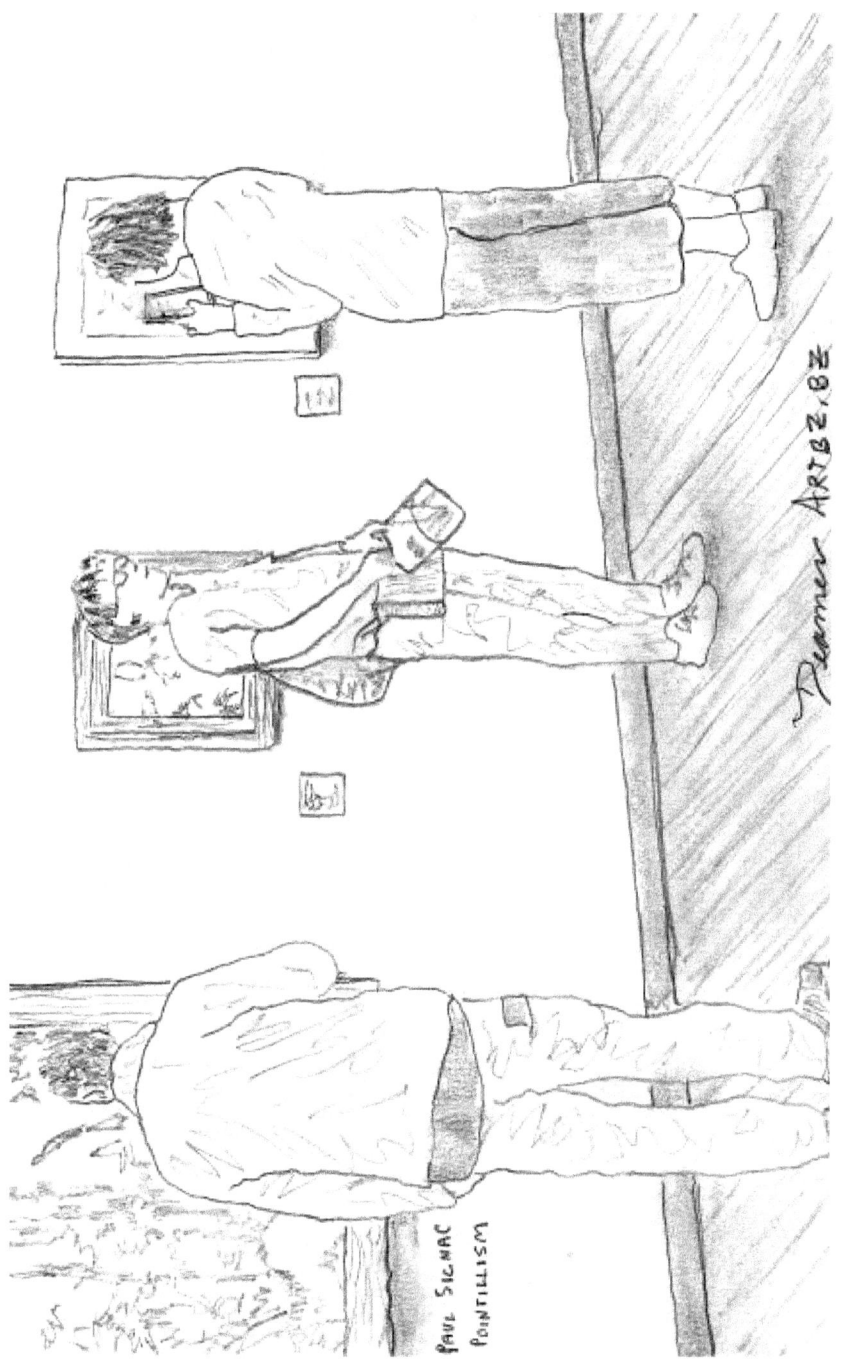

DEAMER DUNN - artbz.bz

INDEX OF ALL THE DRAWINGS

page	sketch		
7	71 Sharing Starry Night	69	28 A Moment of Affection
9	48 First Date	71	29
11	21 Women in Art	73	30 Bear Sculpture
13	61 Selfie Van Gogh	75	31
15	86 Café D'Orsay	77	32
17	1 D'Orsay & The Seine	79	33
19	2	81	34
21	3	83	35
23	4	85	36
25	5 Guadi Exhibition	87	37
27	6 Monet & Family of 3	89	38
29	7 Taking a Break	91	39 Felix Valloton
31	8 Whistler's Ma	93	40
33	9	95	41
35	10 Monet & Threesome	97	42
37	11 Aristide & 3 guys	99	43
39	12 Maillol Sculptures	101	44 Paul Signac
41	13	103	45
43	14 Couple&MaillolSculp	105	46
45	15	107	47
47	16 Ladies	109	49
49	17 Cezanne's Mother	111	50 Monet Haystacks
51	18	113	51 Monet Lillies
53	19 The Bookstore	115	52
55	20	117	53
57	22 Liberty Sculpture	119	54
59	23 Carpeaux	121	55
61	24 Gaugin	123	56 Monet
63	25	125	57 Renoir
65	26 Les Duex Musée	127	58
67	27 VanGogh&Threesome	129	59

SKETCHBOOK – PARIS MUSEE D'ORSAY

131	60	157	75Monet
133	62Girl Sculpture	159	76Warior
135	63HenriToulouse-Lutrec	161	77Pissarro
137	64	163	78
139	65	165	79Cafe Campana
141	66Emily Bernard	167	80
143	67Renoir	169	81Examining
145	68Degas	171	82ImagesinaDarkRoom
147	69	173	83Les Gleaners
149	70	175	84Monet Umbrellas
151	72Van Gogh Church	177	85Student Drawing
153	73Van Gogh	179	87Manet & 2 Couples
155	74HenriToulouse-Lutrec	181	88Signac&PhonePhoto

I began by only labeling these sketches in the order I drew them. I later added some titles to assist you, though, the idea was to set up this book so it could be a bit of a treasure hunt. Exhibitions change; the art is rotated. Thus, you will not find all the works pictured in this book. But you can still have some fun finding some pieces as well as identify some locations within the gallery. The most changing art is the humans which inhabit these pages. I hope you can also amuse yourself imaging stories about some of them, like I did in the fictional tales I open the book with ☺

Deamer Sketchbooks:

In case you haven't heard, coloring books for all ages are becoming quite a passion. Perhaps our ever-complicated world and its demands on our attention are fueling this trend. I think that we all wish that we had more time for reading. For many, perhaps a little coloring can still feed a passion for getting into a book and more easily allow the satisfaction of finishing something. The idea is that this is a book that you can make your own. This series also hopes to be a supplement for travel. Whether you take it along or you allow it to take you.

Available Deamer Sketchbooks:

SAN DIEGO / SAN DIEGO: LITTLE ITALY MERCATO / CENTRAL COAST CALIFORNIA / CHERRYBEAN COFFEE, SALINAS CA / TIJUANA MEXICO (DUAL LANGUAGE BOOK) / UMBRIA, ITALY / SAN FRANCISCO / *MUSEUM OF MODERN ART SAN FRANCISCO* / SKETCH/COOKBOOK PS GRILL / NEW YORK CITY, *MUSEUM OF MODERN ART NYC* / HAVANA CUBA / HONG KONG / MAIN STREET SALINAS / MARKET DAY CARMEL-BY-THE-SEA / SEATTLE / LAS VEGAS / PARIS / *MUSEE D'ORSAY PARIS* / LUGANO SWITZERLAND

Coming Soon:
SALT LAKE CITY / MIAMI / AUSTIN TEXAS / NEW ORLEANS SANTA FE, NEW MEXICO

Being Researched:
BERLIN, VIENNA, PRAGUE, BUDHAPEST, RIO DE JANERIO, BUENOS AIRES, BOGOTA COLOMBIA, SINGAPORE, BANGKOK, TOKYO, INSTANBUL, SOUTH AFRICA, SYDNEY, NEW ZEALAND

SKETCHBOOK – PARIS MUSEE D'ORSAY

Chef Omar T Culinary Adventure Series
TRAVEL FICTION

Omar and his family travel to a different location for each of these culinary adventures. The travel fiction aspect is enhanced with descriptions of actual sites, restaurants, bookstores, galleries and shops—including sketches, favorite lists and recipes. Diversity in race, religion, culture, language and sexual orientation not only exists within Omar's family, it is celebrated in these tales. Each Omar T book is independent, you do not need to read them in the order of their publication, though there are some references for those who do.

Published: Monterey California, San Diego/Tijuana, Umbria Italy, San Francisco, New York City, Havana Cuba, Hong Kong, Seattle, Las Vegas, Paris France, Lugano Switzerland
Coming Soon: Salt Lake City
In the Works: Miami, Austin Texas, New Orleans
Being researched: Santa Fe NM, Madrid, Buenos Aries, Rio, Berlin *and then????*

OMAR T in MONTEREY CALIFORNIA
Omar's Monterey adventures are fed by the literature of John Steinbeck, the eccentricities of Salvador Dali and the amazing beauty and foodstuffs of California's Central Coast.
In Development: Omar T the TV Series!!!

OMAR T in SAN DIEGO & TIJUANA
Omar heads south as his family try to help a San Diego restaurant family survive the sudden death of the father. Omar and his sister's San Diego and Tijuana adventures are fed by the insights of Dr. Seuss, the regions craft beer and food culture, as well as the unique history of these two border cities.

OMAR T in UMBRIA ITALY
Omar joins his mother in Italy where a mysterious fresco reveals itself at the La Romita School of Art. Omar falls for a wine princess and an art restorer. Chapters are organized around each Umbria hilltown that is featured in this book. This allows easy reference for you Umbrian travelers, whether in person or virtually, to use this novel also as a guidebook to this special part of Italy!

OMAR T in SAN FRANCISCO
Omar's investment minded father, creates a partnership for a new San Francisco restaurant with a Beat Generation theme. Omar's whole family gets involved in this adventure, where ghosts of the past swirl around Omar, along with legends from the fifties and sixties San Francisco. Jack Kerouac leads a cast of many Beat writers who rise to color the pages of this modern mystery.

OMAR T in NEW YORK CITY
Omar and his family head to New York City to create a second Restaurant Beat, after successfully launching one in San Francisco. Their vision of centering the restaurant around a performance stage, expands as they get introduced to all the talent of New York musicians, drag queens, comics and eclectic performers. All the fun is tainted by Omar's inadvertent crossing with a Yale secret society.

OMAR T in HAVANA CUBA
Omar and his sister are recruited to participate in a collaboration of international chefs in Havana. They find everything and everyone they encounter a bit mysterious, as they interact with this unique island and its special deities, the Orishas.

OMAR T in HONG KONG
Omar and family head to **Hong Kong** in January 2020 to be the food caterers for the film crew that are remaking the iconic 1960 movie, "The World of Suzie Wong." Omar witnesses the democracy demonstrations, as well as facing a threat of some mystery virus spreading in Wuhan China.

OMAR T in SEATTLE
Omar and his sister head to north to help the Seattle Erotic Art Festival recover from being shut-down by the Covid Epidemic in 2020. The post-pandemic gathering of enthusiasts of the erotic arts in this tech-savvy land of rich green foliage, lakes and a space needle, proves to be exhilarating.

OMAR T in LAS VEGAS
Restaurateur Scott Wynham, CEO of Win&Lose Inc., owner of several Las Vegas hotels and restaurants, feels as if something is wrong within his operations. Omar's father Royce, a friend of Scott, sends Omar to see if by some luck he can discover something. Omar learns that Las Vegas is not only no longer the town of the mob, or even a place dominated by attempts of skimming from its cash business. It is now a land of computers, though it is still a place where people come to reinvent themselves, including attractive young women.

OMAR T in PARIS
Chef Omar heads to the city of love to help with the food service for the film, 'Paris Fourteen.' This collection of short films is shot in each of the first 12 Paris arrondissements, as well as the 14th & 18th. Romance blossoms on and off screen in the city of love.

OMAR T in LUGANO SWITZERLAND
Omar T and Sissy head to LUGANO SWITZERLAND via Sonoma California and Milan Italy, to assist with the food service for Franklin University's 50-year Celebration. This Omar school reunion inspires love and introspection, as Omar returns to his school, more than a decade after its profound influence on his life.

Coming Soon:
OMAR T in SALT LAKE CITY
Omar finds himself in the middle of a kidnapping as well as some interesting Mormon history. Omar and his family's diverse heritage find themselves immersed in yet another culture. One that still finds influence from the times of the Old Wild West—from pioneers to gunslingers.

OMAR T in MIAMI
Omar's artist mother receives one of the Wynwood Walls mural commissions, which inspires her to challenge Omar and his sister to create a cookbook so they can present it at the Miami Book Fair and double as her assistants. Sissy meets a soave Argentinian businessman who introduces her to luxury and Miami eccentricities, while Omar befriends a chain smoking, hard drinking petite New Yorker taking a break from her life as a professional card dealer.

OMAR T in AUSTIN TEXAS
Omar and Sissy are recruited to help with the food service at the Austin Film Festival.

OMAR T in NEW ORLEANS
Omar, Sissy their father and mother, head to New Orleans to assist a Nawlin's restaurant family with their generational challenges.

In the works: MIAMI, NEW ORLEANS, AUSTIN TX, AND SANTA FE NM
Being researched: Berlin, Prague, Vienna, Budapest, Madrid, Singapore, Istanbul, Africa, Rio, Buenos Aires, Sydney, Tokyo and more!!!

Additional Novels by Deamer:

Pickup a Deamer novel online or from your local bookstore:
https://www.amazon.com/author/deamerdunn

STRENGTH AND GRACE

Winner, one of the best fiction novels of 2015,
Southern California Book Festival
Winner, one of the best fiction novels of 2015,
Great Midwest Book Festival

Strength and Grace is the story of a young Mexican woman who stumbles into becoming a bullfighter. She so excels that she becomes a great Matador. The catch is that all but a few think that she is a man. It is a story of female empowerment within the Mexican male culture of the bullfight. There are also coming of age aspects to the story as the reader follows her growth from being a fifteen-year-old tomboy to a twenty-five year old woman who spends the majority of her time being a man. This duality creates identity issues that she must face, along with all of the dangers of her profession and the tension of her masquerade.

Also available in Spanish:
FUERZA y GRACIA (Español)

MEETANDTELL.COM/ADVENTURE

Winner, one of best romance novels of 2016
Los Angeles Book Festival

What is more adventurous than looking for and starting a romantic relationship? Especially with all the new tools and avenues that the Internet has brought to the tips of our fingers. Clark and Ronda's generation began to date before there was a World Wide Web. As they are drawn inside this new magical world, they bring the perspective of experiencing dating before and after the Internet. Two friends in their forties, Clark and Ronda, take us along on their adventure to meet, start and incorporate relationships into their already mature lives. Clark alternates with Ronda in telling their first-person accounts. The story opens with Ronda as a veteran online dater, while Clark reluctantly joins a practice that he sees as belonging to younger generations. What starts as casual fun soon develops into more serious adventure, romance, disappointment and even danger. In a reflection of our time of quick messages, tweets and texts, the chapters are short. They bounce back and forth from the male and female perspectives of Clark and Ronda. This is a story of two people in the timeless pursuit of love during a time of fascinating changes.

Also from Pajaro Street Publishing:

RM Blake EROTICA:
EROTIC REFLECTIONS

This book of erotica includes twenty-two stories, eleven told by a woman, eleven recalled by a man. With illustrations by Deamer.

Also Coming from RM Blake:
THE SEXUAL EDUCATION OF ZOE
AND
THE SEXUAL EDUCATION OF COLIN

These two companion novels mirror each other. Young Zoe approaches her favorite professor to help her further her education.

Colin, like Zoe is also from a difficult background. In this book, his much older professor of philosophy approaches her promising student with continuing his education in her bedroom.

RM Blake Love Song Journals Poignant stories of loss & love

Stephen and Lily

So many of us face addiction, obsession and a drive of compulsion. These drives can create beauty as well as destroy.

Joseph and Mickey

Love later in life can often be complicated. Relationships and history between each lover's families can put a strain on love.

Also Coming Soon:

UMBILICAL CORD A collection of African Stories
Deamer Dunn with co-author/humanitarian

Tererai Trent

*Named by Oprah Winfrey as her favorite all-time Guest!
a collection of African short stories

All Deamer and Pajaro Street books are available wholesale for bookstores and other retailers through both KDP and Ingram.

About the Author/Artist

Deamer is a retired chef/restaurateur who travels the world with his sketchbook and laptop. For each city he visits he creates a Sketchbook (A book to make your own) and a novel with his recurring chef character, Omar T. These are culinary adventure stories he labels "Travel Fiction." Chef Deamer was born and raised in Salt Lake City, Utah. He lived in Switzerland and the Washington D.C. area before settling in Monterey County California in the early 1980's. "I had the incredible luxury of having a world class artist for a mother. Gradually some of her skills rubbed off on me." Deamer maintains a home in the birth city of John Steinbeck, Salinas California, the former location of his dinner only restaurant, Pajaro Street Grill. "I have a list of fifty locations where I hope to write Omar adventures… Come join the journey!"

http://artbz.bz
"Everyday is a great day to read a book or color one!!!"

Keep in touch with Deamer, as Omar travels the world, deamer@artbz.bz Please pass on your impressions; write a review on Amazon and/or other sites such as Goodreads – your thoughts can really make a difference! Just about any bookstore, anywhere in the world, can get you a Deamer book through Ingram at the same price as Amazon ☺ https://www.amazon.com/author/deamerdunn You can also support your local bookstore via: https://bookshop.org/shop/deamerdunn

Romantic, Novelist, Obsessive Traveler, Sketchaholic

À propos de l'auteur/artiste

Romantique, romancière, voyageuse obsessionnelle, Sketchaholic

Je crée un SKETCHBOOK et un roman d'AVENTURE CULINAIRE pour chaque lieu. Les deux livres encouragent les voyages, que vous les emmeniez avec vous ou qu'ils vous emmènent. Ma série SKETCHBOOK est composée de livres destinés à vous faire découvrir le vôtre, vous inspirant de dessins et d'histoires - un livre de coloriage/journal de voyage compagnon pour les adultes. Ma série d'aventures culinaires met en vedette le chef Omar T et sa famille alors qu'ils parcourent le monde en tant qu'ambassadeurs de la diversité et de l'hospitalité. L'aspect fiction de voyage est enrichi de descriptions de sites réels, de restaurants, de librairies, de galeries et de boutiques, y compris des croquis, des listes de favoris et des recettes. Bien que mes romans soient de nature contemporaine, j'aime construire une histoire autour de l'histoire et de la culture réelles d'un lieu. Tout a commencé pour ma famille fictive lorsqu'ils ont fondé un restaurant à Monterey en Californie, décrit de manière similaire au Pajaro Street Grill, que ma femme et moi avons créé en 2019 (RIP mon Nar). Je possède une résidence à l'arrière du bâtiment qui a abrité mon établissement de restauration uniquement pendant vingt ans, à Salinas en Californie, la ville natale de John Steinbeck. s'il vous plaît pardonnez mon horrible français 😊

« Chaque jour est un jour idéal pour lire un livre ou en colorier un !!! »

venez nous rejoindre dans le voyage ! »
http://artbz.bz
https://www.amazon.com/author/deamerdunn

N'importe quelle librairie, n'importe où dans le monde, peut vous procurer un livre de Deamer, via Ingram Publishing.